Table of contents

Introduction — 02

Chapter 1
The Digital Persona — 13

Chapter 2
The Allure of Validation — 30

Chapter 3
The Influence on Relationships — 42

Chapter 4
The Pursuit of Authenticity — 51

Chapter 5
The Darkside of Comparison — 59

Chapter 6
The Cultural Shift — 63

Chapter 7
Deep Fake Technolgy — 79

Chapter 8
Proliferation of Scams — 84

Chapter 9
Cyberbullying and Harassment — 87

Chapter 10
Digital Detox and Well-Being — 97

Conclusion — 104

INTRODUCTION

"**From Likes to Life**: Unraveling the impact of social media, the good and bad," takes readers on a journey through the complex world of social media, examining our identity, influence in relationships, society's mental health, bullying, comparison, validation, detox, cultural shift, and most of all authenticity. The book will delve into the various dimensions of how social media have shaped our world, both positively and negatively.

In the early 2000's, the world witnessed a new technological revolution that changed the way we all connect, communicate, and what we share in in our lives. The evolution of social media can be traced back to the early days of the internet, with the emergence of platforms like Six Degrees, Friendster, and Myspace from the late 1990's and early 2000's. However, it was the launch of platforms like Facebook, Twitter, and YouTube in the mid-2000's that propelled social media into mainstream consciousness, ushering in an era of unprecedented connectivity and communication.

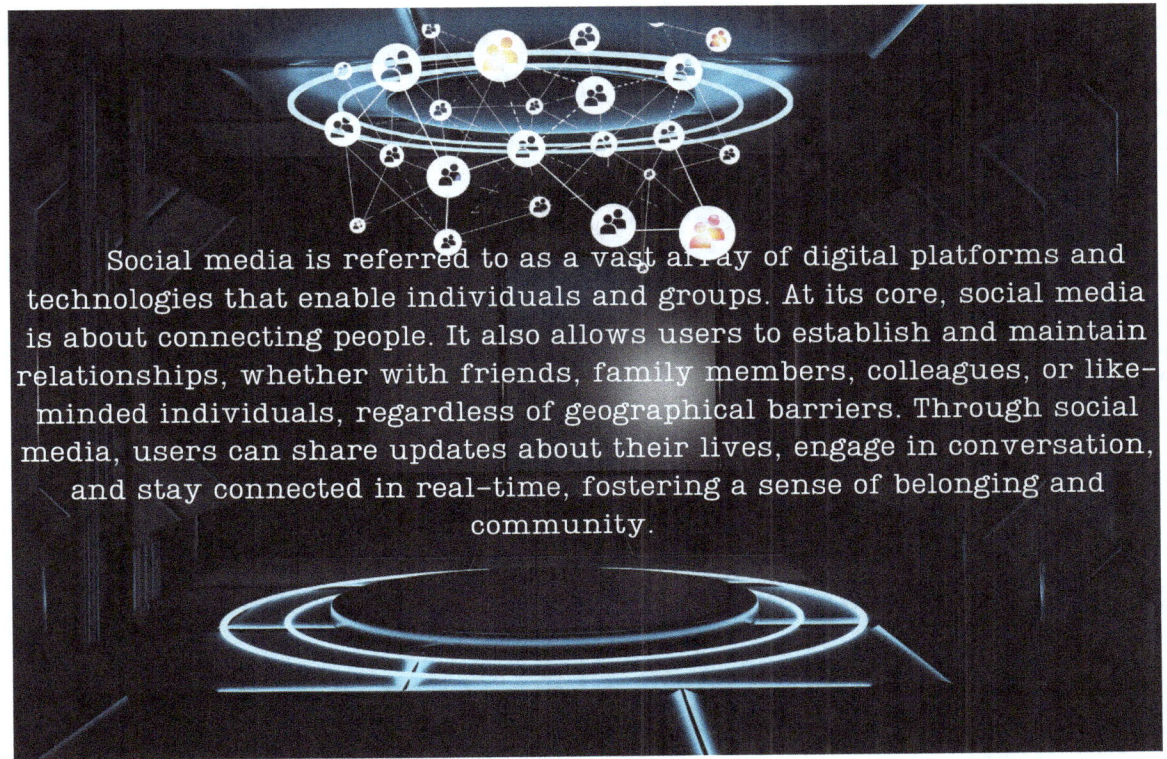

Social media is referred to as a vast array of digital platforms and technologies that enable individuals and groups. At its core, social media is about connecting people. It also allows users to establish and maintain relationships, whether with friends, family members, colleagues, or like-minded individuals, regardless of geographical barriers. Through social media, users can share updates about their lives, engage in conversation, and stay connected in real-time, fostering a sense of belonging and community.

The revolution of social media has been a game changer, for personal and professional growth. It has revolutionized the way we connect, communicate, and interact with one another in the digital age and has become an integral part of daily life for billions of people worldwide.

Social media has undeniably transformed the way we communicate, interact, and perceive the world around us. It's impact on today's society is profound and multifaceted, influencing various aspects of our lives, including social relationship, politics, economics, and culture. However, this impact is not without its complexities and challenges.

There's a wide range of features and functionalities these social media platforms offer, including:

Profile Creation: Users can create personalized profiles with information about themselves, photos, and other media to represent their identities online.

Content Sharing: Users can share various types of content, including text posts, photos, videos, links, and live streams, with their friends, followers, or the public.

Engagement: Social media enables user to engage with content by liking, commenting sharing, or reacting to posts, fostering interaction and community individuals.

Networking: Social media platforms facilitate networking and connections by allowing users to find and connect with friends, family, colleagues, and like-minded individuals.

INTRODUCTION

Communication: Social media platforms offer various communication features, such as private messaging, group chats, voice calls, and video calls, enabling real-time interaction and conversation.

Discovering and Exploration: Users can discover new content, interests, and communities through algorithms, recommendations, hashtags, trending topics, and explore tabs.

Monetization: Many social media platforms offer opportunities for monetization including advertising, sponsored content, subscription, and donations, allowing content creators and business to generate revenue from their online presence.

    Today, social media encompasses a diverse array of platforms, each catering to different types of content, communication styles, and user demographics. Here are some of the platforms that have played a significant role in facilitating communication and connections among loved ones, old friends, colleagues, relationships, and business opportunities:

Facebook: Users can connect with friends, family members, and acquaintances, share update, memes, photos, and videos, and communicate through messages, comments, and video calls and catering to various interest and demographics. Additionally, Facebook Marketplace allows users to buy and sell items locally. Facebook remains one of the most popular social media platforms for staying in touch with family and friends.

YouTube: Allows users to upload, view, and share videos on a wide range of topics and interest. YouTube is currently the largest video sharing platform globally.

WhatsApp: WhatsApp is a widely used app used for messaging and is known for its simplicity and ease of use. It allows users to send text messages, voice calls, video calls, and share photos, videos, and documents with individuals or groups.

Instagram: Instagram, particularly its direct messaging feature, has become popular platform for communication among friends and family, Users can send private messages, share photos, videos, and stories, and engage in real-time conversations with their followers.

TikTok: TikTok is a short-form video-sharing app that allows individuals to create and share videos ranging in different lengths of time, set to music or audio clips. TikTok is also known for its viral challenges, trends, and memes, as well as diverse content spanning comedy, dance, lip-syncing, cooking, educational content, and more. It also offers a wide range of creative tools and effects, including filters, stickers, text overlays, and music libraries, enabling users to produce engaging and entertaining content.

Twitter: Twitter is a microblogging platform where users can share short text-based post, known as tweets, with their followers. Tweets are limited to characters and can include links, photos, videos, hashtags, and mentions. Twitter is also known for real-time updates, news, conversations, and discussions, on various topics, including politics, entertainment, sports, and current events.

LinkedIn: LinkedIn is a professional networking platform used for job searching, recruiting, and business networking. It allows users to create professional profiles, connect with colleagues and industry professionals, and share content related to their field.

Snapchat: Snapchat is a multimedia messaging app known for its ephemeral nature, where messages and photos disappear after being viewed. It features photo and video sharing, stories, filters, and augmented reality lenses.

STREAMING
LIVE

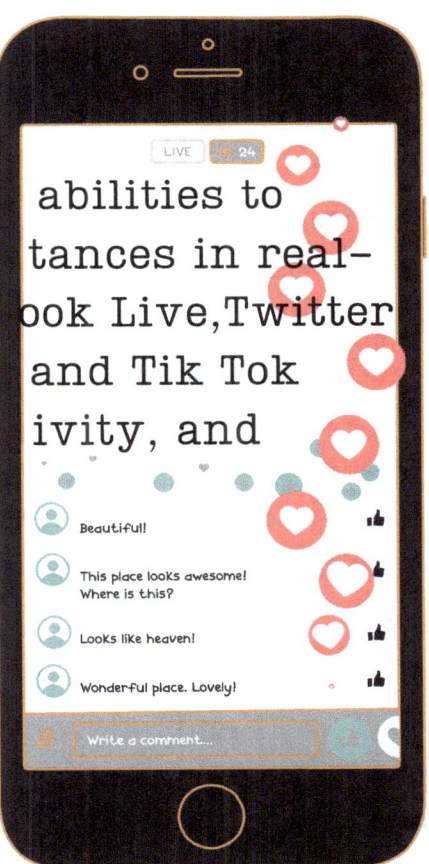

One of the most significant impacts of social media are its abilities to connect people across vast distances in real-time. Platforms such as Facebook Live, Twitter Live, Instagram Live, Discord, and Tik Tok prioritize immediacy, interactivity, and spontaneity, enabling users to engage with content and each other in real-time fostering dynamic and lively social experiences.

CONNECT WITH US ON SOCIAL MEDIA

Social media has reshaped both family dynamics and the landscape of dating, offering opportunities for connectivity, communication, and relationship building while introducing new challenges and considerations. By navigating these complexities thoughtfully and responsibly, individuals and families can leverage social media to strengthen bonds, foster connections, and create meaningful relationships in today's digital world. These platforms have made it easier than ever to stay in touch with friends and family, share experiences, and form democratized information access, and enabling individuals to engage in discussions.

Families that were once separated by miles, could now share everyday moments through photos and videos. Businesses have found innovative ways to reach their customers, and individuals have built personal brands and careers through these platforms.

CONNECT WITH US ON SOCIAL MEDIA

   Social media has become a source of information, education, and even support for those facing various challenges. Social media transcends geographical boundaries, enabling people from different corners of the world to connect, share experiences, and engage in real-time discussions. It has democratized communication on a global scale and is now the primary source of news and information for many individuals that has reshaped the traditional media landscape and provided a platform for citizen journalism.

   Moreover, social media platforms have revolutionized the way business and organizations operate. They serve as a powerful marketing tool, allowing companies to reach a wide audience at a fraction of the cost of traditional advertising. Influencers and brand ambassadors leverage their online presence to endorse products and services, shaping consumer preferences and driving sales.

Additionally, social media platforms have become a virtual marketplace where businesses can directly engage with customers, receive feedback and tailor their offerings to meet consumer demands.

Without social media, social, ethical, environmental, and political ills would have minimal visibility. And because social networks feed off interactions among people, they become more powerful as they grow.

CHAPTER 1
THE DIGITAL PERSONA

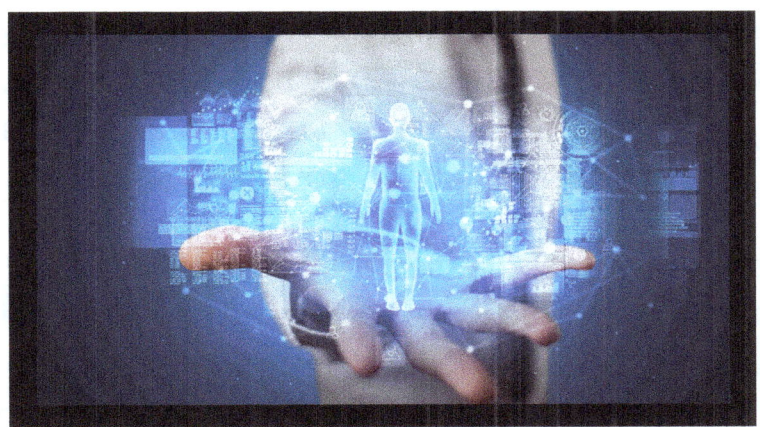

The digital age has become an integral part of our identity, and this phenomenon is encapsulated by the concept of the "digital persona," which refers to individuals that have carefully curated and constructed versions of themselves to present it to the world through social media platforms.

This persona is impacting how we perceive ourselves and how others perceive us and the impact, and significance in today's interconnected world.

From Twitter, Facebook, Instagram and TikTok, they have carefully created curated profiles to filtered photos, individuals who have crafted their online identities and the psychological impact of this digital self-presentation. Digital persona allows access to a global audience.

CHAPTER 1 - THE DIGITAL PERSONA - PROFILE INFORMATION

Your profile information is the foundation of a digital persona that often includes basic information such as name, age, location, and profile picture. These details serve as the initial impression others have of you online.

Social media users carefully select and curate the content they share, creating a narrative that aligns with their desired image. Most social media users choose the most flattering photos, highlighting achievements, and showcasing the most exciting aspects of their life.

This is digital persona which is characterized by "filtered reality." It's a term that refers to the practice of editing and filtering content to present polished, attractive, and an aspirational image. Those filters, photo editing apps, and strategic cropping, are normally used to create an idealized version of that person's life. Yes, this can make the visual content appealing, but it can also blur the lines between reality and fiction.

Understanding the digital persona is essential in navigating the complexities of the digital age, and enabling the world to use social media in ways that align with their authentic selves while maintaining a healthy sense of self-worth.

CHAPTER I - THE DIGITAL PERSONA - NETWORKING

Networking has always been a critical aspect of personal and professional growth, and in the digital age, the concept of networking has extended into the virtual realm.

Through one's digital personal life, networking involves using these online platforms and interactions to connect with peers, colleagues, mentors, and potential collaborators.

With networking, it isn't just about what you can gain, but it is also about what you can contribute. Share your knowledge, offer your assistance, and be valuable resource to your network.

Effective digital networking involves strategic online presence, meaningful interactions, and commitment to building authentic relationships with like-minded professionals and potential collaborators that can enhance one's personal and professional life.

CHAPTER I - THE DIGITAL PERSONA - NETWORKING

Networking on social media has emerged as a pivotal element of personal and professional growth in the digital age. Social media allows individuals to connect with a diverse range of people, exchange ideas, access opportunities, and build relationships in ways that were previously limited to in-person interactions.

These digital platforms enable users to showcase their expertise and interest. Engaging with others through comments, likes, and shares helps establish strong personal brand. Consistent and authentic interaction can attract like-minded individuals and potential collaborators. It also provides tools for business and entrepreneurs to connect with potential customers and clients. Paid advertising, business profiles, and e-commerce features enable business growth.

Social media can be a valuable platform for many users, to connect with others who share similar passions and professional aspirations. It transcends geographic boundaries, allowing for international networking. It empowers users to connect with individuals from various countries, providing a global perspective on industry trends and opportunities.

CHAPTER I - THE DIGITAL PERSONA - NETWORKING

Social media networking fosters collaboration, knowledge sharing, and the pursuit of common goals. Whether it's for career advancement, entrepreneurship, or personal branding, the ability to network online has become an essential skill for leveraging the vast potential of the digital age.

Content creation and monetization are integral aspects of the modern digital landscape, offering opportunities for individuals, business, and creators to share their expertise, entertain audiences, and generate income.

Monetizing social media offers a range of benefits and challenges for content creators and influencers. Some of those benefits are income generation, diverse revenue streams, audience engagement, personal branding and it allows a global reach, reaching a global audience, expanding the potential for income generation and business growth.

Some of those challenges consist of content pressure, audience expectations, competition and income volatility.

Social media monetization offers a path to financial independence and the opportunity to profit from ones' creativity and expertise.

CHAPTER I - THE DIGITAL PERSONA - CONTENT CREATION

In the ever-evolving world of social media, crafting the perfect content cocktail is a well-rounded content strategy that resonates with your target audience on social media platforms. Similar to mixing a cocktail, where various ingredients come together to create a harmonious blend that tantalizes the taste buds, a successful content cocktail combines different types of content to capture attention, foster engagement, and drive results. Content cocktails is finding the right balance of ingredients to stir up a social media sensation.

The percentage provided above (70% syndicated content, 20% curated content, and 10% original content) are commonly cited guidelines that have been used by social media marketers for several years. However, it's important to note that content strategies evolve over time based on changes in audience behavior, platform algorithms, trends and brand objectives.

CHAPTER I - THE DIGITAL PERSONA - CONTENT CREATION

Key ingredients of the content cocktail:
- Original content: Original content serves as the backbone of your content strategy, showcasing your brands' unique voice, expertise, and offerings. This may include blog post, videos, infographics, or product showcases tailored to your audience's interest and preferences.
- Curated content: Curated content adds flavor and variety to your content mix by sharing relevant and valuable content from external sources. This could include articles, blog posts, or industry news that complement hour brand's message and provide additional insights or perspectives to your audience.
- Syndicated content: Syndicated content serves as one of the key ingredients that contribute to the overall mix of content being shared. By incorporating syndicated content alongside other ingredients such as original content, curated content, visual content, and interactive content, brands can create a more diverse and engaging social media presence that caters to the needs and interest of their audience.

Every great cocktail has a distinct taste, and your brands voice is the heart of your content that should be infused with authenticity into every post.

CHAPTER I - THE DIGITAL PERSONA - CONTENT CREATION

By blending these ingredients thoughtfully and strategically, you can craft and create the perfect content cocktail that not only engages your target audience but also drives meaningful interactions, fosters brand loyalty, and achieve your social media marketing objectives. Just as a master mixologist creates a drink that leaves a lasting impression, consistency and your authentic voice helps build trust, fostering a deeper connection with your target audience that can turn your brand into a memorable and engaging presence.

CHAPTER I - THE DIGITAL PERSONA - CONTENT CREATION

Content creation, in its essence, offers both a canvas for creativity and a mirror to society's complexities. On the positive side, content creation empowers individuals and business to express themselves, share their stories, and connect with audiences on a global scale. It democratizes media production, allowing diverse voices and perspectives to be heard and amplified. Content creators can educate, inspire, and entertain, fostering community, empathy, and cultural exchange.

Moreover, content creation has fueled the economic growth through advertising revenue, sponsorship deals, and the monetization of intellectual property, supporting livelihoods and innovation.

Varius platforms and tools are available to facilitate content creation. Content creation spans a wide range of formats, including written articles, blog posts, video, podcast, infographics, social media post, e-books, webinars, and more. Creators choose the format that aligns with their expertise and audience.

Creators use compelling narratives, visuals, and interactivity to captivate and retain viewers, readers, and listeners.

CHAPTER I - THE DIGITAL PERSONA - CONTENT CREATION

With content creation, it also brings challenges and risks. The proliferation of content can lead to information overload, misinformation, and algorithmic bias, making it difficult for audiences to discern truth from fiction. Moreover, the pressure to produce viral content and maintain a constant online presence can contribute to stress, burnout, and mental health issues among creators. Additionally, the commodification of content can prioritize quantity over quality, incentivizing clickbait, sensationalism and shallow engagement. Furthermore, content creation raises some ethical concerns regarding privacy, consent, and the exploitation of vulnerable communities for views and engagement.

While content creation offers a variety of opportunities for expression, connections, and economic empowerment, it is also requiring thoughtful consideration of its impact on individuals, society, and the media landscape. Balancing the good and bad of content creation requires transparency, integrity, and responsible practices to ensure that content serves the greater good while minimizing harm.

CHAPTER I - THE DIGITAL PERSONA - CONTENT CREATION

Despite its potential for connectivity and community-building, social media can also amplify negativity, exacerbate mental health issues, and perpetuate harmful societal norms.

Some social media influencers may engage in the practice of liking or sharing negative content solely to garner attention, likes, retweets, and comments. This behavior can be driven by a desire to increase engagement metrics, boost visibility or capitalize on controversy for personal gain. By associating themselves with negative or controversial content, influencers may attract attention from their followers and exploit algorithms that prioritize engagement metrics. However, this approach can have detrimental effects, contribution to the spread of negativity, misinformation, and toxic discourse on social media platforms.

Social media, at times, can be a breeding ground for negativity, toxicity and harmful behavior. The anonymity and distance afforded by online interactions can embolden individuals to express hostility, engage in cyberbullying, or spread harmful content without consequences.

CHAPTER I - THE DIGITAL PERSONA - CONTENT CREATION

Negative content and online conflicts can escalate quickly, leading to polarization, harassment, and emotional distress for those involved. Moreover, the pressure to maintain a curated and aspirational online persona can exacerbate feelings of inadequacy, comparison, and social isolation among users.

It's essential for users to be mindful of their online interactions, prioritize empathy and kindness, and critical evaluate the content they engage with to foster a healthier and more positive online environment.

CHAPTER I - THE DIGITAL PERSONA - CONTENT CREATION

In today's digital landscape, data privacy is a paramount concern as individuals navigate the complexities of crafting and managing their digital personas. As we engage with various online platforms and services, we leave behind a trail of personal data that encompasses our behaviors, preferences, and interactions. This digital footprint forms the basis of our digital personas, shaping how we are perceived and targeted by companies, advertiser, and algorithms.

However, alongside the convenience and connectivity that digital platforms offer comes the risk of data exploitation and privacy breaches. Concerns about data privacy encompass issues such as unauthorized access to personal information, data mining for targeted advertising, and the commodification of user data without consent.

CHAPTER I - THE DIGITAL PERSONA - CONTENT CREATION

Moreover, the increasing sophistication of data collection techniques and the proliferation of data-driven technologies raise ethical questions about the extent to which individuals have control over their digital identities and the use of their personal data.

As individuals, protecting our data privacy requires awareness, vigilance, and proactive measures. This includes understanding privacy policies, exercising caution when sharing sensitive information online, and leveraging privacy settings and security features to safeguard personal data.

Data privacy is integral to shaping and safeguarding our digital personas in increasingly interconnected and data-driven world. By prioritizing privacy awareness, advocacy, and protection measures, individuals can assert greater control over their digital identities and mitigate the risks associated with data exploitation and privacy infringements.

CHAPTER I - THE DIGITAL PERSONA - CONTENT CREATION

Understanding the role of privacy is essential for navigating the complex landscape of digital interactions, data sharing, and online experiences. At its core, privacy in the digital age is about safeguarding personal data, such as names, addresses, financial records, healthy information and online activities.

Be Mindful of the information you share online. Protect your personal information and ensure you're comfortable with your level of online visibility.

CHAPTER I - THE DIGITAL PERSONA - CONTENT CREATION

The digital persona encompasses profile creation, content creation, monetization, engagement, communication, networking, and discovery and exploration, defining individual's online presence.

Profile creation involves crafting personal profiles with photos and interest, shaping virtual identities. Content sharing empowers users to express creativity, disseminate information, and foster engagement. Monetization opportunities allow content creators to generate revenue through advertising, sponsorship, and merchandise sales. Engagement metrics gauge audience interaction, informing content strategies and driving visibility. Communication features facilitate real-time interaction and relationship building, bridging geographical distances.

Networking enables individuals to expand professional circles, forge partnerships, and access opportunities. Discovery and exploration tools facilitate serendipitous content discovery and trend exploration, enhancing user experience. Together, these elements shape the evolving landscape of digital identity, influencing online interactions and social dynamics.

CHAPTER I - THE DIGITAL PERSONA - CONTENT CREATION

As the digital persons evolve and intersect with real-world identities, ethical considerations, such as privacy, authenticity, and digital well-being, become paramount, shaping the future of online interactions and social dynamics and the understanding of how online identify intersects with real-life identity. With this understanding, it sets the stage for a thought-provoking exploration of how social media has shaped the way we present ourselves to the world. and the profound effects this transformation has on our lives.

CHAPTER 2
THE ALLURE OF VALIDATION

"The Allure of Validation," delves into the psychology behind the pursuit of validation on social media platforms. It explores the powerful role of likes, comments, and shares that has transformed and shaped our self-esteem & self-worth online, addictive behavior, FOMO, mental health challenges, and relationships.

There is a deep desire for humans to be seen, heard, and acknowledged on these social media platforms. Social media platforms have harnessed this basic human need, providing the world with instant feedback mechanisms that trigger the release of dopamine once they receive likes and positive comments.

CHAPTER 2 - THE ALLURE OF VALIDATION

The allure of validation in the digital age is a complex and influential force that stems from our innate human need for social acceptance and recognition.

In the world driven by digital interactions and social media, it's crucial to develop strategies for healthy validation. This involves cultivating a sense of self-worth and well-being that's not solely reliant on external approval or validation from others.

While seeking validation, maintain a healthy sense of self-worth, and prioritize authenticity in our digital interactions. By doing so, individuals can navigate the digital landscape more mindfully and responsibly, enjoying the benefits of validation without becoming overly dependent on it.

The allure of validation often leads individuals to seek immediate feedback and responses to their digital content. Whether it's
a social media post, a blog article, or a video, creators are eager to receive likes, comments and shares.

It's a crucial concept in the digital age, representing the continuous cycle of interaction and response that occurs within the context of online platforms. social media, and digital communication.

CHAPTER 2 - THE ALLURE OF VALIDATION

The pursuit of validation is a powerful driving force behind social media. Every social media platform has created metrics like likes, comments, like and subscribe and shares, which serves as a form of social approval. This provides a sense of affirmation and self-worth, and users often gauge their self-worth based on the number of likes their post receives, followers, and engagement on post.

For some users, with every like, comment, one's popularity, attractiveness, success and shares, there might be a release of dopamine, the "feel-good" neurotransmitter that comes with each notification reinforcing the desire for validation, sometimes leading to compulsive posting, and checking of social media.

Consequently, a lack of validation can lead to feelings of inadequacy, while high engagement can boost one's self-esteem. This neurological response reinforces our pursuit of validation, making it a rewarding and sometimes addictive endeavor.

CHAPTER 2 - THE ALLURE OF VALIDATION

Forms of Digital Validation:

- **Likes to Reactions:** Getting likes or reactions on social media posts can provide a quick sense of validation. It signifies that others have acknowledged and appreciated your content.
- **Comments:** Meaningful comments and feedback from others can offer more substantial validation Constructive comments and engagement can boost confidence and self-worth.
- **Followers and Subscribers:** Growing one's follower count or subscriber base is often seen as a form of validation. It suggests that others find your content, opinions, or expertise valuable.

The Impact of Validation:

- **Positive Reinforcement:** Positive validation reinforces desired behaviors and content sharing. It encourages individuals to continue posting and engaging on social media
- ***Self-Worth and Self-Esteem:*** Receiving validation can positivelg influence an individual's self-worth and self-esteem, contributing to a sense of achievement an belonging.

The Darkside of Validation:

- **Dependency:** An overreliance on digital validation can lead to dependency, where individuals' self-worth becomes contingent on external approval.
- ***Validation Chasing:*** Some individuals become so consumed by the pursuit of validation, often sacrificing authenticity and genuine self-expression to cater to popular trends or opinions.
- **Negative Validation:** Negative comments or criticism can have a detrimental impact on one's mental health, leading to self-doubt, anxiety, and stress.

CHAPTER 2 - THE ALLURE OF VALIDATION - PSMU

Social media addiction, often referred to as problematic social media use (PSMU) or social media dependency, is a phenomenon characterized by excessive and compulsive engagement with social media platforms, to the extent that it in interferes with daily functioning and well being.

Several factors can contribute to the development and perpetuation of social media addiction, such as psychological factors, social factors, design and features of social media platforms, individual vulnerabilities, consequences of social media addiction, and addressing social media addiction.

Social media platforms are designed to trigger dopamine, release in the brain's reward system through likes, comments, shares, and other forms of social validation. This reinforcement mechanism can create a cycle of pleasure-seeking behaviors, similar to that observed in substance addiction.

CHAPTER 2 - THE ALLURE OF VALIDATION - PSMU

It shares similarities with other forms of behavioral addiction, such as gambling or gaming addiction. Individuals with social media addiction often displays symptoms such as:

Preoccupation: Constantly thinking about social media, checking for updates, and feeling anxious when unable to access it.

Loss of Control: Difficulty limiting the time spent on social media despite attempts to cut back, leading to neglect of responsibilities, work, or personal relationships.

Withdrawal Symptoms: Experiencing negative emotions, irritability, or restlessness when unable to use social media.

Negative Impact: Social media addiction can lead to adverse effects on mental health, including increased stress, anxiety, depression, and decreased self-esteem. It can also interfere with offline relationships, productivity, and well-being.

Escapism: Using social media as a way to escape from real-life problems, or emotions, leading to a cycle of dependency.

Compulsive Behavior: Engaging in social media activities compulsively, such as constantly refreshing fees, seeking validation through likes and comments, or comparing oneself to others.

CHAPTER 2 - THE ALLURE OF VALIDATION - PSMU

For some individuals, social media serve as a means of escape from real-life stressors, loneliness, or negative emotions. The instant gratification and distraction provided by social media can temporarily alleviate discomfort but may lead to reliance and dependency over a period of time.

CHAPTER 2 - THE ALLURE OF VALIDATION - FOMO

In today's digital world, FOMO, or Fear of Missing Out is a driving force behind the pursuit of validation. It is driven by the digital age and the constant connectivity provided by our smartphones, social media, and the internet.

FOMO describes the apprehension or anxiety individuals experience when they believe they are missing out on experiences, events, or opportunities, especially those happening online or through these social media platforms.

FOMO even extends to professional domains, where individuals may worry about missing out on job opportunities, promotions, or experiences that could further their careers. People often feel pressured to stay updated with digital content.

CHAPTER 2 - THE ALLURE OF VALIDATION - FOMO

It is driven by the constant stream of content, social comparison, and the wealth of opportunities provided by technology. The primary driver of FOMO is the tendency to compare one's life to others, especially through social media. Individuals often perceive their own experiences as less exciting or significant in comparison to what they see on their social media feeds.

In today's digital world, there are an abundance of options, but time and resources are limited. FOMO arises when individuals must choose among various activities, fearing they will make the wrong choice.

Managing FOMO involves developing self-awareness, mindfulness, setting boundaries for social media use, practicing gratitude for what one has, and prioritizing meaningful offline experiences and connections. By focusing on personal values and goals rather than comparing oneself to others, individuals can reduce the impact of FOMO and cultivate a greater sense of contentment and fulfillment in their lives. It can help you become aware of your validation-seeking behaviors and make conscious choices in the digital realm. Also, pay attention to how certain content makes you feel and whether it contributes to your well-being or detracts from it.

CHAPTER 2 - THE ALLURE OF VALIDATION - DIGITAL LOOP

The digital loop of social media describes the continuous cycle of engagement and feedback that users experience when interacting with online platforms. It begins with users consuming content, such as a posts, video, or images, shared by others in their social network.

As users engage with this content by liking, commenting, or sharing, they provide feedback that reinforces the behavior of both the content creators and themselves. This feedback serves as validation and encourages users to continue participating in the platform, perpetuating the cycle.

CHAPTER 2 - THE ALLURE OF VALIDATION - DIGITAL LOOP

The digital feedback loop provides this immediate feedback. As soon as content is published, the loop generates engagement data, including likes, comments, and shares, offering creators, the validation they seek.

This loop has far-reaching implications, shaping how individuals and organizations engage with digital content and how information spreads across the internet.

Once the content is created, it's published or distributed on various online platforms, websites, or social media channels.

This content can reach a vast and often global audience, thanks to the internet's reach.

Social media users, including individuals and organizations, are engaging with the content in various ways. This engagement includes actions like liking, sharing, commenting, and reacting to contents.

CHAPTER 2 - THE ALLURE OF VALIDATION - DIGITAL LOOP

Mindfulness involves being present in the moment without judgment. It can help you become aware of your validation-seeking behaviors and make conscious choices in the digital realm.

Establish clear boundaries for screen time, both terms of the duration and the activities you engage in. Reducing the amount of time spent on social media can reduce the pressure to seek constant validation.

By shaping the social norms to prioritize authenticity and offline experiences, we can mitigate the negative impact of PSMU and FOMO and create a healthier digital and mental environment.

CHAPTER 3
THE INFLUNCE OF RELATIONSHIPS

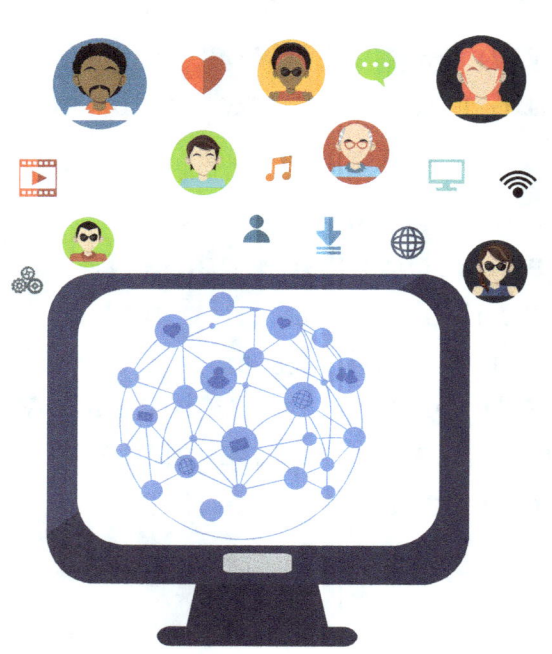

Social media has transformed the dynamics of human relationships around the world, touching every aspect of our personal and professional lives. It serves as a bridge that connects us with friends, family, colleagues, and even strangers across the globe.

As these social media platforms evolve, the influence of relationships becomes increasingly integrated into our daily existence. Social media has not only redefined how we communicate but has also expanded the horizons of friendship. Strangers, united by common interests, shared experiences, or empathy, can now form genuine, meaningful connections online.

However, it is essential to approach these connections with a degree of caution while acknowledging the potential for genuine, authentic, friendships to emerge from the digital realm.

CHAPTER 3 - THE INFLUENCE OF RELATIONSHIPS

One remarkable aspect of social media is it can reconnect individuals with old friends, family, or acquaintances from various phases of life. Whether it's reuniting with childhood friends, rediscovering college buddies, or reconnecting with former colleagues, these platforms have made it possible to rekindle or maintain relationships that might have otherwise faded over time.

In many cases, social media has been a lifeline for those in long-distance relationships. It's not about exchanging messages, but it's about sharing experiences, seeing each other's faces, and feeling a sense of presence when miles apart.

Social media has revolutionized the way people form connections, enabling strangers to become friends in ways previously unimaginable.

This transformation is at the heart of the digital age, reshaping the dynamics of human interaction, community-building, and friendships. It has transcended geographical boundaries, allowing individuals from different corners of the world to connect. Users can find and interact with like-minded individuals, sparking the formation of friendships that would have been unlikely without these digital platforms.

CHAPTER 3 - THE INFLUENCE OF RELATIONSHIPS

Many social media groups and forums provide spaces for individuals to seek support and empowerment. Strangers unite over shared challenges, such as health issues or personal struggles, forming deep connections and friendships based on empathy and understanding.

Social media platforms have also witnessed spontaneous acts of kindness where strangers offer help, support, or encouragement to others in need. These moments can lead to development of meaningful friendships based on compassion and shared values.

Ultimately, social media has the potential to bridge gaps and foster friendships between people from diverse backgrounds, cultures, and experiences. Online platforms can challenge stereotypes and prejudices, enabling understanding and empathy to flourish.

Professionals and creatives find social media to be a valuable space for collaboration and networking. Strangers with complementary skills or interest can come together to work on projects, share ideas, and establish professional relationships that may evolve into friendships.

CHAPTER 3 - THE INFLUENCE OF RELATIONSHIPS - FAMILY

The influence of social media is an evolving topic that has become an integral part of modern life, and its effects on family relationships, communication, and interactions have become increasingly significant.

Many families have been influenced by social media and it has allowed many families to stay connected and involved in each other's lives especially if they are separated by geographical distances. It facilitates real-time communication through messages, video calls, and sharing updates, fostering a sense of togetherness.

On the flip side, over-reliance on digital communication can sometimes replace face-face interactions within the family. It may lead to reduced quality time spent together, affecting the depth of family relationships.

Social media provides a platform for families to share significant life moments, achievements, and experiences. For some families, it has strengthened their family bond and have allowed relatives to participate in each other's lives, even when far apart.

However, it can present its challenges, such as generational gaps in understanding the nuances of digital communication and etiquette. For example, some parents and grandparents may have different perspectives on privacy and sharing, which could lead to occasional conflicts.

CHAPTER 3 - THE INFLUENCE OF RELATIONSHIPS - FAMILY

Also, over-sharing personal family moments can raise concerns about privacy and security issues could also become a negative impact with it comes to social media. There is a balance to be stuck between celebrating family events and maintaining personal boundaries.

Children and teenagers may also engage with social media without a full understanding of the potential dangers. Parents should have discussions about online safety that will be crucial to protecting your family members from cyberbullying, harassment or inappropriate content.

The impact of social media on family is a complex interplay of positive and negative influences. It has the potential to enhance communication, strengthen bonds and offer valuable resources for parenting. The key is to approach social media use within the family with mindfulness, open communication, and a balanced approach to maintain healthy and supportive relationships while leveraging the advantages of digital connectivity.

CHAPTER 3 - THE INFLUENCE OF RELATIONSHIPS - DATING

The impact of social media on relationships is a multifaceted phenomenon that has both positive and negative implications for personal, romantic, and even professional relationships.

Social media platforms provide a vast pool of potential romantic partners, expanding the dating pool beyond geographical boundaries. Dating apps like Tinder, Bumble, and Hinge leverage social media profiles to match users based on shared interest, mutual friends and location. Its offering new ways to connect and find love. Messaging features on social media platforms enable individuals to initiate conversations and get to know each other before meeting in person, facilitating smoother and mor efficient communication.

These social media platforms provide avenues in navigating relationships and defining the relationship (DTR), making it "Facebook official," for individuals to declare their relationship status, their love for one another, milestones, such as engagement, weddings, or anniversaries. While this can be seen as a source of joy and celebration, it can also place pressure on individuals to conform to societal norms and expectations regarding relationships.

CHAPTER 3 - THE INFLUENCE OF RELATIONSHIPS - DATING

Social media profiles serve as a digital resume, allowing individuals to curate and showcase aspects of their personality, interests, and lifestyle. Profile pictures, bios, and posts contribute to the initial impression and attractiveness perceived by potential partners. However, the curated nature of social media profiles could lead to misrepresentation or exaggeration of one's traits, hobbies, or accomplishments, potentially setting unrealistic expectations or leading to disappointment when meeting offline.

Dating etiquette and norms is shaping expectations regarding communication frequency, response times, and digital interaction boundaries. Ghosting, breadcrumbing, and orbiting are behaviors that have emerged in the digital dating landscape. Additionally, social media provides opportunities for public displays of affection (PDA's), such as liking, commenting, or tagging partners in post, which can reinforce relationship dynamics and validate the connection in the eyes of others.

CHAPTER 3 - THE INFLUENCE OF RELATIONSHIPS - DATING

Relationships are a big part of our lives, and some social media relationships are in a disarray. While social media can enhance romantic relationships in many ways, it also presents several challenges that couples need to navigate. Some of these challenges can affect the dynamics, trust, and overall health of romantic relationships.

Some couples air their relationship problems publicly on social media. This not only exposes intimate details, but can also lead to public breakups, which can emotionally be challenging and invasive.

Couples may have different views on what should remain private and what can be shared on social media, and this can lead to disagreements when one partner shares
aspects of the relationship that the other would prefer to keep private.

And there are those social media relationships that other's view, can impact the commitment in another relationship, which could lead to betrayal and possibly the demise of the relationship.

Social media could be very dangerous if unchecked. Too many relationships face betrayals as a result to social media.

CHAPTER 3 - THE INFLUENCE OF RELATIONSHIPS

The influence of social media on relationships is undeniable. It has the potential to enhance connectivity, strengthen friendships, and even help people find love.

Social media have bridged geographical gaps, making it easier for individuals in long distance relationships to stay connected through video calls, instant messaging, and sharing personal updates.

To navigate the digital connection successfully, individuals should be mindful of the impact social media may have on their relationships and implement healthy communication and boundaries to maintain strong authentic connections in both their personal and professional lives.

CHAPTER 4
THE PURSUIT OF AUTHENTIFAKECITY

Society in today's world is dominated by social media's idealized images and curated content, the pursuit of authenticity that has emerged as a powerful countercultural force.

The desire to embrace authenticity in the digital ages is a response to the superficiality and perfection that is often portrayed on all these social media platforms.

Authenticity should begin with honesty and unvarnished storytelling that involves sharing not only the highlights but also the lows and challenges of life. One that acknowledges perfections and vulnerabilities fosters a sense of relatability and genuine connections with others.

The pursuit of authenticity often leads to vulnerability, which might seem paradoxical in a digital landscape that may see vulnerability as weakness.

CHAPTER 4 - THE PURSUIT OF AUTHENTICITY

    While the pursuit of authenticity is commendable, it is not without some challenges. Those that are authentic may feel apprehensive about sharing their vulnerabilities, fearing judgement or backlash.
    However, sharing ones' vulnerabilities can create powerful connections because those individuals will open up about their struggles, fears, and insecurities and they too will invite others to do the same.
    Navigating those challenges may require self-awareness and understanding of one's boundaries. Life is not always picture -perfect, and imperfections are a part of the human experience.

CHAPTER 4 - THE PURSUIT OF AUTHENTICITY

Authenticity on these social media platforms is complexed a nuanced phenomenon. While many individuals strive to be authentic and genuine with their online interactions, the nature of these platforms often presents challenges and incentives that can affect how affect how people portray themselves. For example, those users who use their social media platform to motivate, they aim to share their authentic experiences thoughts, and emotions, while other users may seek validation, recognition, or even financial gain through their influencer status.

CHAPTER 4 - THE PURSUIT OF AUTHENTICITY- LIVING DOUBLE LIVES

The phenomenon of living a double life on social media is a complexed and multifaceted one. It involves individuals who present a stark contrast between their online personas and their real-world identities.

Living a double life on social media is rooted in the duality of online and offline identities. People often create carefully curated persona on these social media platforms that may not accurately reflect who they are in real life, and it can be influenced by a various of factors.

Motivations for creating a double life may include escapism. Individuals try and escape from their real-world problems or to distance themselves from their true identity. They may also create idealized persona to cope with personal issues.

Another motivation would be the desire for acceptance and the need for validation. Acceptance can drive people to craft idealized online persona that garner likes, followers, and admiration, fulfilling and emotional void in their lives.

You also have those individuals that may experience a double life due to aspirations and insecurities. Double lives can stem from aspirations and insecurities.

CHAPTER 4 - THE PURSUIT OF AUTHENTICITY- LIVING DOUBLE LIVES

Individuals may present themselves as more successful, attractive, or adventurous than they feel they are in reality. Last but not least, anonymity is also part of a double life.

The cloak of online anonymity can embolden some individuals to adopt entirely different personalities, often for harmful or deceptive purposes. The selective presentation of life events, experiences, and emotions on social media enables individuals to curate the image they want to project, amplifying the divide between their online and offline selves.

Social media platforms can foster echo chambers where like-minded individuals reinforce and validate the double life, making it difficult for the individual to step out of the facade.

CHAPTER 4 - THE PURSUIT OF AUTHENTICITY- LIVING DOUBLE LIVES

There are consequences of living a double life. Trying to maintain a double life can lead to stress, anxiety, and a sense of inauthenticity, as individuals constantly struggle to keep up appearances.

It can also damage personal and professional relationships with family, friends, and even colleagues who may feel deceived or hurt when they discover the discrepancy between online and offline persona.

And in some cases, when the truth is emerged, some individuals may become targets of cyberbullying and harassment, as their deceitful behavior can provoke negative reactions from others.

CHAPTER 4 - THE PURSUIT OF AUTHENTICITY- ALGORITHMS

JUST BE YOU

Let's not forget about the impact of algorithms. The algorithms on these social media platforms are profound and far reaching and play a pivotal role in shaping the user experience and its influencing various aspects of our digital lives.

Algorithms are the hidden engines that power the content we see, the connections we make, and the interactions, we have on these platforms. Social media algorithms analyze the data you use and your behavior and curate it to personalize your content fees. What does this mean? It means that what one user sees will differ significantly from what another user sees. It tracks the engagement metrics of the user such as like, comments, shares, shares and click through rates. Nowadays, people almost post anything on their social media page whether it be the truth or lie..

Authenticity on these social media platforms does exist on a spectrum, while there are various factors including personal motivation, social pressures, and algorithms influences that can impact the degree of authenticity.

In all honesty, authenticity is a personal choice that is influenced by an individual's values goals, and comfort levels.

CHAPTER 4 - THE PURSUIT OF AUTHENTICITY

Authenticity is a valuable currency, shaping personal relationships, branding, and the credibility of content. It encourages individuals to be true to themselves, share their stories, and connect with others on a more human level.

The pursuit of authenticity has become a significant cultural and personal imperative as individuals, brands, organizations aimed to present themselves with transparency and integrity in an online landscape characterized by diverse forms of content and communication. It is a reminder that social media often presents a curated version of reality, and that authentic self-expression is valuable. It underscores the importance of self-awareness and the need to promote a culture of authenticity and empathy in the digital age, recognizing that the gap between one's online and offline self can have significant consequences for individuals and their relationships.

Maintaining authenticity in a digital world can be challenging, but it's essential for fostering trust and creating meaningful connections with an audience.

CHAPTER 5
THE DARKSIDE OF COMPARISON

It is undoubtedly that social media has brought about many positive changes, but it also cast a shadow, giving a rise to a range of issues and challenges in our everyday lives. This chapter, we will explore the detrimental habit of social comparing and how it can affect individuals of all ages and backgrounds. But if we understand its origins, mechanisms, and what to watch out for, the world will be able to mitigate the negative effects and amplify the good both online and offline.

CHAPTER 5 - THE DARKSIDE OF COMPARISON

Social comparison and envy are deeply rooted in psychological phenomena that have gained new dimensions in the digital age of these social media platforms and online interactions. They have fostered unrealistic comparison, jealousy, and sense of inadequacy among users. These experiences have far reached effects on individuals' self-esteem, mental well-being, and relationships. Social comparison can be both objective and subjective.

Objective comparison involves tangible metrics, such as income and physical appearance. Subjective comparisons are influenced by individuals' personal interpretation and perceptions.

Envy arises when those individuals compare themselves to others they perceive as having something they lack, whether it's success, possessions, or attributes. Envy can manifest as feelings of resentment, inadequacy, or bitterness.

CHAPTER 5 - THE DARKSIDE OF COMPARISON

People often compare themselves to those they perceive as having more desirable qualities, possessions, or experiences. When individuals are posting content on social media, they tend to selectively present the best aspects of their lives on social media, showcasing achievements, milestones, and happy moments and the viewers perceive a skewed reality.

These social media platforms foster a culture of comparison, where users constantly measure their lives against the curated and idealized content of others which could lead to feelings of inadequacy, envy, and isolation and that is a growing concern.

When an individual believe that one has more money, acclaim, looks, followers, home(s), career, or whatever, the spike of envy they trigger is natural.

All of the social media platforms are primed to amp it up. Don't be fooled and be misled and internalize the belief that you are not measuring up to the idealized images and lifestyles that you see online.

Comparing oneself can contribute to negative self-perception and low self-esteem causing anxiety, depression, suicidal thoughts, life dissatisfaction and psychological distress.

CHAPTER 5 - THE DARKSIDE OF COMPARISON

Excessive social comparison, especially on social media, is linked to negative mental health outcomes, including increased stress, depressive symptoms, and decreased life satisfaction.

If envy is affecting one's mental health, it may be helpful to seek support from friends, family, or a mental health professional. Talking about one's feelings can provide validation and coping strategies. Engage with like-minded individuals that can provide a sense of belonging and it will reduce feelings of isolation. Since comparison is fundamental human, there's really no way of shutting it down.

I encourage to practice self-awareness and cultivate gratitude for your own experiences and strengths.

> Social comparison and envy are complex psychological phenomena exacerbated by the digital age and social media.
> They can have a significant impact on an individual's mental health and overall well-being.
> Recognizing the dynamics of social comparison and envy, promoting mindful consumption of social media, and fostering culture of authenticity and support can contribute to more positive and emotionally healthy environment.

CHAPTER 6
THE CULTURAL SHIFT

The cultural shift catalyzed by social media is nothing short of revolutionary. These digital platforms have not only transformed the way we communicate but have irrevocably altered our society, from the way we interact with one another to the way we define our identities, consume entertainment, engage in politics, and even conduct business.

This digital landscape, fueled by social media and the interconnectedness of online communities, has given rise to a vibrant and ever-evolving culture of viral trends, internet challenges, advertising, entertainment, memes, fashion, humor, and new forms of language.

These phenomena have transformed the way we communicate, express humor and engage with digital content. Social media has undeniably played a pivotal role in shaping popular culture.

CHAPTER 6 - THE CULTURAL SHIFT

Social media is also conditioning our minds and shaping unreasonable expectations. For example, if everyone is going with the trend, you have others following and doing the same thing wanting to be "liked or right."

These social media platforms are so powerful, they are interfering with people's thinking. Example of interference is, someone can post something, and that person have a lot of likes, there are some people who will trade in the truth for a lie just to get more likes. In this digital age, people will also do and say whatever they feel is trending. Just because something is trending, doesn't always mean it is the truth, liked or right.

From livestreams to blogs, to photography, social media can have multiple effects on people, and it doesn't matter where you are in the world.

There is endless power when it comes to the internet and social media. So many people have been able to prove their creativity with that power.

Instant connectivity has allowed social media to redefine communication by enabling instant connectivity with people across the globe.

CHAPTER 6 - THE CULTURAL SHIFT

Visual content in the form of images, video, and emojis has become a fundamental part of communication. Memes and GIFS have become cultural phenomena, offering nuanced ways of expressing emotions and ideas.

The rise of platforms like Snapchat and Instagram, stories introduced the concept of ephemeral content. These temporary updates have changed the way we share moments and narratives, emphasizing the fleeting nature of digital interactions.

Social media platforms are catalysts for amplifying trends. A single video or post can quickly gain popularity, prompting countless users to mimic, adapt, or reinterpret the trend and those trends can spread globally in a matter of hours.

CHAPTER 6 - THE CULTURAL SHIFT

Social media have created a world of expectations and leaving so many people globally unsatisfied due to a five-to-ten-minute viral content. Some people actually base their lives off of individuals content that in some cases are unrealistic.

Platforms like Instagram have popularized the idea of the "highlight reel," where individuals share their best moments and achievements, often presenting a skewed version of reality. And this too can create an unrealistic expectations and foster feelings of inadequacy. People are curating moments, instead of living in the moment.

The cultural shift catalyzed by social media is nothing short of revolutionary. These digital platforms have not only transformed the way we communicate but have irrevocably altered our society, from the way we interact with one another to the way we define our identities, consume entertainment, engage in politics, and even conduct business.

CHAPTER 6 - THE CULTURAL SHIFT

This digital landscape, fueled by social media and the interconnectedness of online communities, has given rise to a vibrant and ever-evolving culture of viral trends, internet challenges, advertising, entertainment, memes, fashion, humor, and new forms of language.

These phenomena have transformed the way we communicate, express humor and engage with digital content. Social media has undeniably played a pivotal role in shaping popular culture.

Social media is also conditioning our minds and shaping them with unreasonable expectations. For example, if everyone is going with the trend, you have others following and doing the same thing wanting to be "liked or right."

Some people really believe that all "influencers" are really influencers. All influencers are not influencers. We live in an age where people are wanting fame, and influence is what they think they are doing for the sake of wanting lots of people to validate them as individuals.

In this cultural shift, people are put on a pedestal, infatuated with, and idolized for details that most times don't exist. Remember, all influencers are not influencers.

CHAPTER 6 - THE CULTURAL SHIFT

However, there are those influencers that believe people are supposed to give them attention without working for it.

In the realm of social media influence, the practice of content appropriation or "content stealing" unfortunately exist, where some influencers may repurpose or share content from other influencers without fact-checking or proper attribution. This behavior can stem from various motivations, including the desire to capitalize on trending content, maintain a consistent posting schedule, or simply lack of awareness about intellectual property rights and ethical considerations.

One common scenario involves influencers reposting or sharing viral content without verifying its accuracy or original sources. In their eagerness to capitalize on popular trends or engage their audience, influencers may overlook the importance of fact-checking and due diligence, leading to the dissemination of misinformation or unverified claims. This can potentially harm both the original content creator, who may not receive proper credit or recognition for their work, and the audience, who may be misled by inaccurate or incomplete information.

CHAPTER 6 - THE CULTURAL SHIFT

In addition to ethical concerns, content appropriation can also have legal implications, as it may violate copyright laws or intellectual property rights. Content creators have the right to control how their work is used and distributed, and unauthorized use of copyrighted material can result in legal action or penalties.

To address this issue, it's essential for influencers to prioritize integrity, transparency, and respect for intellectual property rights in their content creation and sharing practices. This includes fact-checking information before sharing it with their audience, obtaining permission or properly crediting sources when using others' content, and fostering a culture of collaboration and mutual respect within the influencer community. By upholding ethical standards and best practices, influencers can help build trust with their audience and contribute to a healthier and more responsible social media ecosystem.

Social media have shifted from creating content to creating content tailoring content for algorithms. Maximizing engagement and views has become the ultimate goal, leading to clickbait headlines, with manipulated images, and fast-edited vides.

CHAPTER 6 - THE CULTURAL SHIFT

Clickbait on social media refers to content, typically headlines or thumbnails, designed to entice users to click through to a website or view a piece of content. Clickbait often employs sensationalist language, provocative imagery, or misleading claims to grab attention and generate clicks. While clickbait can drive traffic and engagement, it can also have several negative impacts on individuals and the broader online ecosystem.

Clickbait often relies on deception or exaggeration to lure users into clicking on content. This can erode trust between content creators and their audience leading to skepticism and cynicism towards online content. In some cases, clickbait headliners may misrepresent or exaggerate the content of an article or video, leading to the spread of misinformation and fake news. Those users who click on the clickbait may be exposed to inaccurate or biased information, contributing to confusion and polarization.

CHAPTER 6 - THE CULTURAL SHIFT

Some content clickbait creators rely on manipulative tactics to exploit psychological vulnerabilities and trigger impulsive behavior. By appealing to users' curiosity, fear, or desire for novelty, clickbait can encourage clicks even when the content is of little value or relevance.

It's essential for content creators, platforms, and users to prioritize transparency, authenticity, and integrity in their online interactions. Content creator should strive to provide value to their audience through high-quality, hones, and engaging content, while platforms should implement measures to identify and demote clickbait content in their algorithms. Additionally, users should exercise critical thinking and skepticism when encountering clickbait on social media, taking the time to verify information and consider the credibility of the sources before clicking or sharing.

CHAPTER 6 - THE CULTURAL SHIFT

    The dynamic evolution continues to impact every facet of our lives, posting both opportunities and challenges that demand our ongoing consideration and adaption in the digital age.

    As we navigate this cultural shift, it is essential to maintain a critical awareness of its influences and consequences, while fostering a responsible and empathetic digital culture.

    The digital culture shift has evolved around social media platforms and online communities that is marked by the rapid propagation of
viral trends, engagement in internet challenges, the widespread of memes, a unique sense of humor, and the development of a distinct online language.

    These elements have fundamentally reshaped the way we interact, communicate, and express ourselves in the digital world. These elements are not only a source of entertainment but also a means of fostering connection, expression, and shared experiences in the digital age bringing people together in new and innovative ways.

CHAPTER 6 - THE CULTURAL SHIFT

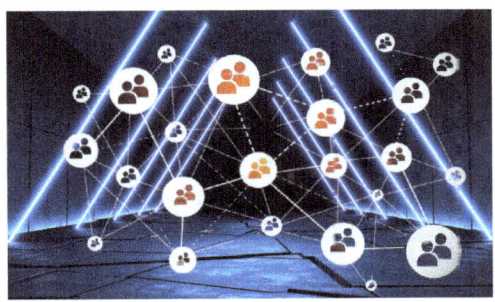

The cultural shift includes the transforming of communication. It allows instant connectivity and social media has ushered in an era of instant connectivity, where individuals can engage in real-time conversations and share their experiences with a global audience.

The geographical boundaries that once restricted communication have been virtually erased. This transformation has bought about the visual language, which is the use of visual content, including images, videos, and emojis, that have become an integral part of online communication.

Memes and GIF's are powerful tools for conveying humor and emotions. Platforms like Snapchat and Instagram have introduced the concept of ephemeral content, where post disappear after a short time. This dynamic has also shaped the way people share their lives, emphasizing the transient nature of digital interactions.

Influence on entertainment and media is also a part of the cultural shift. Social media profoundly influences music and video trends, catapulting songs to stardom and bringing attention to viral videos. TikTok, in particular, has played a pivotal role in this phenomenon.

CHAPTER 6 - THE CULTURAL SHIFT

The transformation of the way movies, TV shows, and streaming content shared on social media, allows the sharing of trailers,
behind-the-scenes content, fan theories, and fan communities have been formed and is instrumental in building anticipation.

Social media platforms have revolutionized how political information is distributed. Politicians can now communicate directly with voters, an ordinary citizens can engage in citizens journalism, breaking news stories in real time.

With the personalized algorithms of social media, it can create filter bubbles, where users are primarily exposed to content that aligns with their existing beliefs, which can lead to echo chambers and the polarization of political discourse.

Memes are humorous or satirical cultural symbols, often in the form of images, videos, or text, that convey a message. They can go viral very quickly, thanks to their relatability, humor, or social commentary.

Internet humor frequently relies on shared experiences and references that resonate with a broad audience. The humor can be absurd, ironic, or rooted in self-deprecations.

CHAPTER 6 - THE CULTURAL SHIFT

You ever wonder about those internet challenges? Internet challenges have become a prevalent form of online interaction, where individuals or groups engage in specific activities with unique twist or creative angle, and then share their experiences on social media platforms for fun or social awareness.

There's a variety of challenges on social media and some of those challenges encourage user engagement and participation and often go beyond online spaces, with users taking part in real-world activities, filming themselves, and then sharing their experiences.

While many of these challenges are light-hearted and harmless, some can pose a significant risk to participant. However, there are dangers to some of these internet challenges that may have raised safety concerns, as participants might engage in risky behaviors.

You have the physical type of challenge that involves physical actions that can be hazardous. For example, the "Fire Challenge" encouraged individuals to set themselves on fire, resulting in severe injuries.

CHAPTER 6 - THE CULTURAL SHIFT

Participants may not fully comprehend the risks associated with such challenges. Then you have those that are doing these challenges due to peer pressure.

Those individuals have the desire to fit in and be accepted which can lead them to participate in challenges they would not otherwise consider.

Peer pressure, especially among adolescents and young adults, can influences risky decision making. Some challenges involve illegal activities and engaging in such
challenges can lead to legal ramifications.

While internet challenges can be a source of entertainment and social interaction, it's crucial to approach them with caution. Participants should be aware of the potential dangers and exercise critical thinking when deciding to partake in these activities.

CHAPTER 6 - THE CULTURAL SHIFT - OVERVIEW

The cultural shift of social media has been profound, fundamentally altering how individuals interact, consume information, and perceive the world around them. Initially heralded as a tool for connectivity and democratized communication, social media platforms have evolved into influential cultural forces that shape behavior, attitudes, and societal norms in unprecedented ways.

One of the most significant cultural shifts brought about by social media is the rise of digital communities and virtual identities. Social media platforms have facilitated the formation of online communities based on shared interest, beliefs, and identities, transcending geographical boundaries and traditional social structures. This has fostered a sense of belonging and solidarity among divers groups, while also enabling the rapid dissemination of information and mobilization for social causes. Moreover, social media has democratized content creation and distribution, empowering individuals to share their voices, perspectives, and creativity with global audiences. Usher-generated content, influencer marketing, and viral trends have reshaped cultural consumption patterns, challenging traditional media gatekeepers and amplifying underrepresented voices and perspectives.

CHAPTER 6 - THE CULTURAL SHIFT - OVERVIEW

However, the cultural impact of social media is not without its challenges and controversies. Issues such as misinformation, echo chambers, cyberbullying, and digital addiction have emerged as pressing concerns, highlighting the darker side of online connectivity and the need for responsible digital citizenship.

Overall, the cultural shift of social media reflects a complex interplay between empowerment and exploitation, connection and isolation, democratization and polarization. As social media continues to evolve, it will undoubtedly shape and be shaped by broader cultural dynamics, influencing how we communicate, collaborate, and construct our collective identities in the digital age.

CHAPTER 7
DEEP FAKE TECHNOLGY

Deepfake technology, a powerful application of artificial intelligence (AI), has garnered significant attention due to its ability to create hyper-realistic but fabricated images, videos, and audio recordings. The term "deepfake" is derived from "deep learning," a subset of AI that utilizes neural networks to mimic human behavior and appearance with astonishing accuracy. This technology has a wide range of applications, from entertainment and creative storytelling to more controversial uses like misinformation and identity theft.

Deepfakes are typically created using Generative Adversarial Networks (GANs), where two AI models- the generator and the discriminator-work in tandem. The generator creates fake content, while the discriminator evaluates it against real data.

CHAPTER 7 - DEEPFAKE TECHNOLOGY: AN IN-DEPTH EXPLORATION

This process enables the creation of video where individuals appear to say or do things they never actually did, with their likeness and voice convincingly mimicked. The ability to manipulate visual and auditory content has led to concerns about the spread of misinformation, political and social contexts.

Deefakes can be weaponized to undermine trust, create fake news, or harass individuals by placing them in compromising situations that never occurred.

CHAPTER 7 - DEEPFAKE TECHNOLOGY: AN IN-DEPTH EXPLORATION

In the age of social media, where attention spans are short, and content consumption is rapid, AI-powered video editing has become a game-changer. These tools allow creators to produce polished, engaging videos quickly, making it easier to capture the fleeting attention of online audiences.

Social media has evolved from a simple platform for sharing likes and comments to an intricate ecosystem that deeply influences various aspects of our lives. In this transformation, AI and new technologies have played a pivotal role, particularly in how content is created, shared, and consumed.

The integration of AI-generated characters, animation, and video editing tools has not only redefined how we interact with social media but has also blurred the lines between digital and real life.

The integration of AI-generated characters, animation, and video editing tools has not only redefined how we interact with social media but has also blurred the lines between digital and real life.

CHAPTER 7 - DEEPFAKE TECHNOLOGY: AN IN-DEPTH EXPLORATION

On one hand, it can create compelling, innovative content that pushes the boundaries of creativity. On the other, it poses serious risks related to misinformation and identity theft.

- **CREATIVE STORYTELLING:** Deepfakes can be used creatively to craft unique narratives, bringing historical figures of life, or allowing celebrities to engage with fans in new and unexpected ways. On social media, this can translate to viral content that garners widespread attention and engagement.

- **THE DARK SIDE:** However, the same technology can be misused to spread misinformation, create false identities, or manipulate public opinion. In a world where likes and shares often equate to credibility, the potential for deepfakes to distort reality is a profound concern.

CHAPTER 7 - DEEPFAKE TECHNOLOGY: AN IN-DEPTH EXPLORATION

In summary, the implications of deepfakes extends to legal and regulatory challenges as well. Determining the authenticity of media and protecting individuals' rights to their likeness are becoming increasingly complex issues.

As deepfake technology advances, the need for robust detection tools, public awareness, and legal frameworks to address the potential harms becomes ever more critical. Balancing the creative possibilities of deepfakes with their potential for misuse will be a key challenge in the digital age.

CHAPTER 8
PROLIFERATION OF SCAMS

Social media is a powerful force in today's world, profoundly shaping how we connect, communicate, and perceive reality. While it offers numerous benefits, such as instant communication, access to information, and the ability to build communities, it also comes with significant drawbacks–one of the most pressing being the prevalence of scams and the negative impacts they can have on individuals. Social media platforms have become the breeding grounds for various types of scams, including phishing, identity theft, fake investment schemes, fake accounts and fraudulent e-commerce.

The proliferation of scams on social media has become a significant concern as these platforms grow increasingly integral to our daily lives. Scammers leverage AI and other advanced technologies to create highly convincing and sophisticated schemes, targeting individuals and businesses alike. Social media vast reach and the trust users place in their networks make it a fertile ground for such activities.

CHAPTER 8- PROLIFERATION OF SCAMS

　　AI-driven tools enable scammers to automate their efforts, making it easier to target large numbers of people with personalized messages that appear legitimate. For example, AI can generate fake profiles, craft convincing messages, and even mimic the voices or appearances of trusted individuals using deepfake technology.

This creates a significant challenge for both users and platform administrators, as distinguishing between genuine and fraudulent content becomes increasingly difficult.

　　Scammers exploit the anonymity and wide reach of these platforms to target individuals, often using sophisticated methods to appear legitimate. With minimal oversight and rapid information spread, these scams can quickly ensnare large numbers of victims.

CHAPTER 8- PROLIFERATION OF SCAMS

Social media is a powerful force in today's world, profoundly shaping how we connect, communicate, and perceive reality. While it offers numerous benefits, such as instant communication, access to information, and the ability to build communities, it also comes with significant drawbacks-one of the most pressing being the prevalence of scams and the negative impacts they can have on individuals.

The impact of these scams can be devasting, leading to financial losses, reputational damage, and psychological distress for victims. As scammers become more sophisticated, the need for robust security measures and user education is critical. Social media platforms are implementing AI based detection systems to identify and block fraudulent activities, but these measures must continually evolve to keep pace with the ever-changing tactics of scammers.

For users, being vigilant, questioning the authenticity of online interactions, and being aware of the latest scam techniques are essential steps in protecting themselves from falling victim to these schemes.

CHAPTER 7
CYBERBULLYING AND HARASSMENT

Social media platforms, while designed to facilitate communication, networking, self-expression, and connection, also serves as arenas where individuals can display the worst aspects of their behavior.

Online bullying and harassment have become disturbingly common on all these social media platforms.

Both are disturbing manifestations of mean-spirited behavior that have found a breeding ground on these platforms. The extreme meanness witnessed on social media is a complex phenomenon rooted in various psychological, social, and technological factors.

Cyberbullying and harassment, along with mean-spirited behavior, is representing the disturbing underbelly of the digital age.

"The perpetrator doesn't get a chance to see how damaging their bullying is and how to learn from their mistakes and do something different."

CHAPTER 7 -CYBERBULLYING AND HARASSMENT

Enabled by technology and the anonymity of the internet, these behaviors inflict emotional, psychological, and sometimes physical harm on individuals.

Social media cyberbullying is just as harmful, and perhaps even worse, than in person bullying. It can happen at anytime and anywhere.

The internet along with these social media platforms, while offering myriad opportunities for connection and communication, also serves as a breeding ground for a darker side of human interactions.

Cyberbullying often takes the form of sending or sharing harmful or mean content about someone to embarrass them. Sometimes this content is shared anonymously, which makes cyberbullying feel even more threating. The fact that perpetrators hide behind screens does not make the effects of cyberbullying and less damaging to those involved.

The physical separation of individuals in the online world from those they interact with can result in less empathy and reduced inhibition against negative behavior.

When people interact behind the safety of a screen name or avatar, they often feel detached from their real-world identities. This anonymity creates a sense of invisibility and a reduced sense of accountability for their actions.

CHAPTER 7 -CYBERBULLYING AND HARASSMENT

It can lead individuals to express thoughts and emotions they might never share with face-to-face interactions.

In the age of social media, the platforms are a breeding ground for opinions and perspectives. Some may offer constructive feedback, while others express disagreement.

People should agree to disagree. It is understood that if one is not part of the solution, they are the problem. On many of these platforms, there are those individuals who responds negatively or in a mean-spirited way to a post, is operating in their own trauma or their truth consuming toxicity. There are a lot of individuals who do not know how to process their emotions and is causing some of the toxicity that is overflowing in our digital world.

"The perpetrator doesn't get a chance to see how damaging their bullying is and how to learn from their mistakes and do something different."

CHAPTER 7 - CYBERBULLYING AND HARASSMENT

Unfortunately, the online world is also rife with those who resort to harassment, cyberbullying or toxic comments. It may begin with and innocently intended post. This could be a comment, a photo, or a status update shared on the platform. The person that shared the post or update, may have various motivations to express an opinion, share a personal moment, or engage a lighthearted conversation.

The conflict may spill into targeted harassment. As the feud intensifies, individuals may start to engage in online harassment by consistently sending hurtful messages, threats, or derogatory comments. A lot of social media users will throw a rock and hide behind their hand. Instead of focusing on the message, the harassers will focus on the messenger.

This can severely impact the target's mental and emotional well-being, leading to anxiety, depression, or other psychological distress.

CHAPTER 7 -CYBERBULLYING AND HARASSMENT

With the online world of harassment, it can take a more sinister turn with the practice of "doxxing." This involves exposing personal information such as addresses, phone numbers, or workplace details. Armed with this information, harassers can threaten, intimidate, or even physically stalk their targets. Believe it or not, the online world and the real world are increasingly interconnected.

When harassment reaches an extreme level, it can spill over into an individual's offline life. Those offline harassments could be physical threats where the harasser may use physical threats or engage in stalking, causing genuine fear and safety concerns for the target.

If and individual post or comments, and the harasser(s) don't agree, it is wrong for the harasser(s) to stalk the target at their home, work, school or any place the target visits. This could cause physical harm and could lead to someone's life whether it be the target or harasser(s). It's okay to disagree without wanting to harm an individual.

Nobody's safety should be on the line whether it is online or offline. Individuals should have restraint and understanding.

"The perpetrator doesn't get a chance to see how damaging their bullying is and how to learn from their mistakes and do something different."

CHAPTER 7 - CYBERBULLYING AND HARASSMENT

There is also the impact on relationships which those individuals targeted may face strained personal relationships as friends, family members, or colleagues become aware of the harassment. In some cases, harassment may involve one's employment or education.

Online harassment can affect's one's professional and educational life. Employers and schools are increasingly taking online actions into account, which are leading to disciplinary actions or even job loss or expulsion.

"The perpetrator doesn't get a chance to see how damaging their bullying is and how to learn from their mistakes and do something different."

CHAPTER 7 - CYBERBULLYING AND HARRASMENT

Understanding why people exhibit such behavior is essential to address the negative impact it has on individuals and communities. Here are some factors that may contribute to cyberbullying, harassment and toxicity on social media.

THE POWER OF ALGORITHMS

Social media platforms use algorithms that prioritize content that generates engagement. This often means controversial or extreme content is more likely to appear on users' feeds.

When individuals encounter polarizing or sensational posts repeatedly, it can foster a culture where extreme opinions and meanness becomes more socially acceptable.

Algorithms are integral to how social media platforms operate, shaping the content we see, the ads we encounter, and the overall user experience.

"The perpetrator doesn't get a chance to see how damaging their bullying is and how to learn from their mistakes and do something different."

CHAPTER 7 - CYBERBULLYING AND HARRASMENT

Echo Chambers and Confirmation Bias

Social media platforms often curate their online experiences by following like-minded individuals and groups. This creates echo chambers, where they're exposed primarily to content that aligns with their existing beliefs. This insulation can lead to confirmation bias, where people reject opposing views and can become increasingly entrenched in their own, often extreme, perspectives. Consequently, they may respond to different viewpoints with meanness.

Frustration and Anger

Some individuals use social media as venting outlet for their frustrations and anger. They might target strangers or acquaintances, releasing their negative emotions in the form of saying meanness things.

Insecurity and Jealousy

Insecure individuals may lash out at others due to feelings of inadequacy or jealousy. They project their own insecurities onto others, resorting to mean spirited comments as a way to cope with their own emotional turmoil.

"The perpetrator doesn't get a chance to see how damaging their bullying is and how to learn from their mistakes and do something different."

CHAPTER 7 - CYBERBULLYING AND HARRASMENT

 The social media revolution represents a significant shift in the way people connect, communicate, and share information.

 As it continues to evolve, it brings both opportunities and challenges, necessitating ongoing reflection, innovation, and regulation to ensure its positive impact on the world.

 Cyberbullying can be in many forms, including personal attacks, harassment or discriminatory behavior, spreading defamatory information, misrepresenting oneself online, spreading private information, social exclusion and cyberstalking. When online harassment escalates to physical threats, stalking, or doxing, legal action should be taken.

> "The perpetrator doesn't get a chance to see how damaging their bullying is and how to learn from their mistakes and do something different."

CHAPTER 7 - CYBERBULLYING AND HARRASMENT- OVERVIEW

In summary, the journey from a social media post to online or offline harm, is a complex and distressing process. The interconnectedness of the online and offline worlds means that a seemingly harmless digital interaction can lead to tangible, and detrimental consequences.

This underscores the need for responsible online behavior, robust privacy settings, and a commitment to fostering a safer, and more compassionate online environment.

Allow this as a reminder of the potential harm that can result from the misuse of these digital platforms and the importance of promoting a culture of respect, empathy and love online.

"The perpetrator doesn't get a chance to see how damaging their bullying is and how to learn from their mistakes and do something different."

CHAPTER 8
DIGITAL DETOX AND WELL-BEING

DIGITAL DETOX

Globally, most of us spend more time than we'd like to admit glued to our phone, tablets, or any electronic device. And there is no denying that there are some benefits from these social media platforms. However, the use of technology is affecting so many individuals mental health.

Have you ever thought about how much time is spent on checking your phone to check personal and or work emails, respond to messages, and check social media? Studies have found that most individuals spend at least 8 hours of screen time on cell phones, tablets, computer screens, and TV screens. And many do not realize just how much time they are dedicating to these electronics.

CHAPTER 8- DIGITAL DETOX AND WELL-BEING

The digital age has now become an integral part of our lives, and the need for occasional detoxing has grown in importance. The time spent scrolling through social media and the constant connectivity, notifications, and information, is causing a digital overload.

The constant exposure to curated lies and social media comparison is contributing some anxiety, low self-esteem, and other negative emotions globally.

As the influence of social media continues to grow and shape our lives, it's crucial to explore how we can navigate the future while harnessing its potential benefits and addressing it challenges.

Social media's impact on mental health becomes more evident, it is vital to promote Digital Detox and Well-being.

After engaging on social media, and you experience any of these, you might need to
take a digital detox from social media.

- Anxiety, stress or depression after scrolling on social media
- Social withdrawals
- Feeling obligated to respond immediately
- Disrupted sleep
- Urge to check your phone or electronic device every few minutes

CHAPTER 8- DIGITAL DETOX AND WELL-BEING

What is a digital detox? It is a conscious break from digital devices and online platforms aimed at fostering well-being and balance in the digital age. The benefits of digital detox are numerous and extended to various aspects of an individual's life.

A digital detox is what you want it to be. In life, we all should set some type of boundaries and setting digital boundaries is vital to one's health. Do what is best for your lifestyle. The importance of setting digital boundaries, is finding balance between the virtual and the real world to enhance your overall wellbeing.

DIGITAL DETOX REFELCTIONS

CHAPTER 8- DIGITAL DETOX AND WELL-BEING

For every scroll or swipe, it sends a hit of dopamine to the same areas of your brain that responds to addictive and dangerous drugs. Digital detox should be a part of a larger strategy for achieving digital balance and long-term well-being.

While you are digital detoxing, inform family and friends about the detox plan and enlisting their support and understanding. Doing a digital detox doesn't necessary mean cutting off all digital contact but maintain essential communication channels while eliminating non-essential digital distractions.

There is a need for ongoing awareness of one's tech habits and the willingness to make adjustments as needed.

> Pay attention to your emotions when you scroll on social media. Are you bored? Do you need it for work? Do you feel like you are missing out on something or what others have? Does checking your phone make you feel better or worse. Getting a sense of your emotions will allow you better control over the use of your phone. While doing a digital detox may present some challenges, it does offers numerous benefits for mental health, sleep quality, and overall well-being. The key is to set clear boundaries, plan meaningful offline activities, and reflect on the experience to make long-term changes that promotes a healthier relationship with social media and digital technology.
>
>

CHAPTER 8- DIGITAL DETOX AND WELL-BEING

There are benefits of temporally disconnecting from the digital world to recharge and regain perspective. Here are some of those benefits.

- **Improved Mental Health:** Digital detox alleviates feelings of stress, anxiety, and emotional overwhelm associated with the constant digital presence. It offers individuals a reprieve from the pressure of maintaining a digital persona and responding to notifications.
- **Increased Productivity**: Digital detox frees up time and energy, redirecting it towards more productive and fulfilling activities. In some cases, some individuals have rediscovered their passions, hobbies, and interest, leading to increased overall productivity.
- **Reconnection with Real Life:** By disconnecting from screens allows individuals to fully engage in face-to-face interactions, nurturing and strengthening relationships with family and friends. This reconnection with the physical world fosters authentic human connections.
- **Balancing Relationships:** A digital detox allows individuals to balance their relationships, giving priority to real-life connections. It can strengthen the quality of these relationships by promoting genuine face-to-face interactions.
- **Improved Attention and Focus:** Break free from the constant interruptions of notifications and emails. By doing this, it leads to improved attention and focus, which is crucial for task requiring deep concentration.
- **Personal Growth:** The time and mental space regained through digital detox can be channeled into personal growth and self-discovery. Individuals often find themselves reevaluating their priorities and values, leading to positive and personal development.
- **Stress Reduction:** Reducing digital distractions and the constant stream of information that the online world offers can significantly reduce stress levels, allowing individuals to experience a greater sense of calm and relaxation.
- **Enhanced Digital Consciousness**: Experiencing a digital detox provides individuals with a valuable perspective on their digital habits. This heightened awareness enables more conscious and mindful use of digital devices and online platforms in the future.

DIGITAL DETOX REFELCTIONS

- Reevaluating Digital Habits: Reflect on how technology is used and making intentional choices about its role in your life.
- Challenges of a Digital Detox: Fear of Missing out (FOMO) - During detox, one may worry about missing out on important updates, news, or social events.
- Post-Detox Reflection: After your detox, reflect on how it impacted your well-being, relationships, and overall quality of life.
- Long -Term Digital Well-being: Individuals should consider incorporating regular digital detoxes into their routines, such as weekly breaks or seasonal detoxes. Setting boundaries for screen time can contribute to long-term digital well-being.

CHAPTER 8- DIGITAL DETOX AND WELL-BEING - OVERVIEW

Despite the increased connections, relationship building, and the ability to stay in touch with friends and family, social media's addictive nature has negatively affected our society since its inception.

Whether you feel your experience with social media is positive or negative, doing a digital detox can undoubtedly be a game changer and refreshing from time to time.

A digital detox is a powerful tool for regaining balance and well-being in the digital age. It offers a respite from the constant demands of screens and the online world, allowing individuals to experience enhanced mental health, improved sleep quality, increased productivity, and deeper connections in both their digital and physical lives and it brings awareness of time and energy spent on network.

CHAPTER 8- DIGITAL DETOX AND WELL-BEING

In this digital world with cell phones, or any electronic devices, people are no longer engaging with in pure conversation. People are on their electronic devices while eating, walking, watching television or chatting while with another person.

Disconnecting from your screens, allows individuals to fully engage in face-to-face interactions and it strengthens relationships with family and friends. This connection with the physical world fosters authentic human connections.

A study has found that over 70% of individuals reported using their phones every night before bed, which was correlated with poor sleep quality and mood dysfunction. Getting an adequate amount of rest is essential to maintain overall health, and getting poor sleep can even have adverse effects on the body itself. Do your body a favor and be kind to your mind.

OVERVIEW AND CONCLUSION OF "FROM LIKES TO LIFE"

"From Likes to Life," Unraveling the Impact of Social Media, The Good and Bad, explores the transformative influence of social media on individuals and how it is changing the trajectory globally.

Since the evolution of these social media platforms, everyone wants their voice to be heard. The book offers a comprehensive examination of the role of social media in modern life, highlighting both its benefits and drawbacks. It delves into the positive aspects, such as connectivity, activism, and personal branding, as well as the challenges.

OVERVIEW AND CONCLUSION OF "FROM LIKES TO LIFE"

These extensive summaries provide a deeper understanding of the key topics related to social media and its impact on individuals in society as a whole.

The Digital Persona:

The digital persona is the identity that individual create and project in the online world, often through social media. It is a carefully curated representation of themselves, allowing them to express creativity, connect with others, and shape their online presence. While it offers opportunities for self-expressions and communication, it can also lead to issues of authenticity and blurred lines between the digital and real-world selves.

The Allure of Validation:

The Allure of Validation in the context of social media refers to the strong desire for approval, recognition, and positive feedback from one's online presence. Social media platforms offer instant gratification in the form of likes, comments, and shares fulfilling the human need for social validation.

However, this pursuit of validation can lead to addiction, self-esteem issues, and a constant need for external affirmation.

OVERVIEW AND CONCLUSION OF "FROM LIKES TO LIFE"

The Influence of Relationships:

Social media platforms influence on relationships is multi-faceted and have a profound impact. It facilitates connections, communication, allowing individuals to maintain relationships across distances.

However, it can also introduce complexities, including misunderstandings jealousy, and privacy concerns. Social media has allowed us to be more aware and engaged in the lives of those we care about, including our spouses or partners. In today's society, you can now share your relationship with the world.

With technology now, it does have its pros. But one cannot deny that there are cons and those cons have come with some problems. One of the most important relationships starts with family. With so much new technology, family bonding is no longer part of family lives. Prior to the revolution to these social media platforms, families would gather together face-to-face and meaningful conversations after a day's work at home of just unwinding.

Families barely greet one another, and you see everyone engrossed in their phones watching videos, reacting to post online, scrolling on social media, or responding to friends that may have become more important on social media.

OVERVIEW AND CONCLUSION OF "FROM LIKES TO LIFE"

The Influence of Relationships:

Social media as allowed us to be more aware and engaged in the lives of those we care about, including spouses or partners. Social media has also made it possible for the individuals to share their relationships with the world. This can be both positive and negative, too.

For some, sharing too much on social media can lessen intimacy in a relationship, and sharing too little could very well cause others to question the authenticity of it.

If you are going to be sharing your relationships on social media platforms, find a balance between sharing too much and not sharing enough is important to a healthy relationship.

OVERVIEW AND CONCLUSION OF "FROM LIKES TO LIFE"

The Pursuit of Authenticity:

The pursuit of authenticity in the digital age revolves around the desire for genuine self-expression and the presentation of one's true self online.
Many users seek to break away from the prevailing culture of curated personas by striving for authenticity. However, this pursuit
can also generate pressure and challenges, as individuals grapple with the expectation of being true to themselves who may be having identity struggles.

The Dark Side of Comparison:

The dark side of comparison on social media revolves around the prevalent tendency to compare oneself to others based on their online posts and achievements. This behavior can lead to feelings of inadequacy, envy, and negative impact on self-esteem. It highlights the need for individuals to engage in mindful and healthy online interactions.

OVERVIEW AND CONCLUSION OF "FROM LIKES TO LIFE"

The Cultural Shift:

The cultural shift brought about by social media signifies the transformation of how society communicates, shares information, and engages with one another. It has redefined cultural norms, values, and trends shaping the way we share and consume content. this shift underscores the profound impact of digital culture on contemporary society.

Deepfake Technology:

Deepfake technology presents a complex blend of opportunities and risks in the digital era. While it offers creative possibilities in fields like entertainment and education, the potential for misuse is significant, particularly in spreading misinformation, manipulating public opinion, and violating personal privacy. As deepfakes become more advanced and harder to detect, the challenge lies in developing effective safeguards–such as improved detection tools, public education, and legal frameworks–to protect individuals and society from the harmful consequences of this power technology. Balancing innovation with ethical responsibility will be essential as we navigate the future of deepfakes.

Proliferation of Scams:

The proliferation of scams, especially on social media, underscores the growing complexity and sophistication of digital threats in today's world. With AI enabling more convincing and widespread fraudulent activities, users are increasingly at risk of financial loss, identity theft, and emotional harm. The vast reach and inherent trust in social media platforms make them prime targets for scammers, necessitating heightened vigilance, user education, and the implementation of advanced security measures. As these scams continue to evolve, it is crucial to stay informed and proactive in protecting ourselves and our digital communities from these pervasive threats.

Cyberbullying and Harassment:

Cyberbullying and online harassment refer to harmful behaviors on digital platforms, including threats, insults, or the spread of false information. These actions can lead to emotional distress, mental health issues, and even physical harm. Addressing cyberbullying is a pressing societal challenge that underscores the importance of promoting a safer and more empathetic online environment.

OVERVIEW AND CONCLUSION OF "FROM LIKES TO LIFE"

Digital Detox and Well-being:

Digital detox involves intentionally disconnecting from technology, especially social media, to improve mental and physical well-being. It recognizes the potential negative consequences of excessive screen time, such as reduced productivity, disrupted sleep, and heightened stress. A well-executed digital detox can lead to enhanced mental health, improved focus, and stronger relationships.

OVERVIEW AND CONCLUSION OF "FROM LIKES TO LIFE"

The digital persona, cultivated through likes and interactions on social media, has become a central aspect of modern identity. Users carefully curate their online persona, selecting content that reflects their desired image and garners validation from their peers. The allure of validation drives individuals to seek approval through likes, comments, and shares, often equating social media engagement with personal worth and validation. Relationships are influenced by social media, with interactions and connections increasingly mediated through digital platforms.

While social media facilitates communication and connection, it can also foster superficial relationships and detract from meaningful, face-to-face interactions.

Amidst the pursuit of authenticity, social media users grapple with the pressure to present an idealized version of themselves online. The relentless pursuit of perfection breeds anxiety and insecurity, fueling the dark side of comparison. Users constantly compare themselves to others, leading to feelings of inadequacy, jealousy, and low self-esteem. The cultural shift brought about by social media has reshaped societal norms and behaviors, influencing everything from communication styles to beauty standards.

OVERVIEW AND CONCLUSION OF "FROM LIKES TO LIFE"

However, alongside its positive aspects, social media also harbors darker elements. Cyberbullying and harassment thrive in the online realm, with individuals facing abuse, threats, and discrimination behind the veil of anonymity. The anonymity afforded by social media can embolden perpetrators, exacerbating the psychological toll on victims. In response to these challenges, digital detox and well-being initiatives have emerged, encouraging users to unplug and prioritize their mental health. Digital detox involves taking breaks from social media to reduce stress, improve focus, and foster offline connections.

In conclusion, while social media offers unprecedented connectivity and opportunities for self-expression, it also presents complex challenges and risks. Understanding the nuances of the digital persona, the allure of validation, and the influence of relationship is crucial for navigating the digital landscape responsibly. By fostering authenticity, promoting empathy, and prioritizing well-being, individuals can harness the positive potential of social media while mitigating its negative impacts.

"From Likes to Life" provides a comprehensive overview of this landscape, emphasizing the importance of responsible and mindful engagement with digital platforms in the pursuit of a balanced and fulfilling digital life.

![Social Media puzzle with terms: Like, Online, Rank, Friends, Share, Networking, Internet, Blog, Partnership, Reputation, Chat, Connection, Recommend, Www, Content, Marketing, Tweets, Follow, Relationship, Community, Advertising, Communication]

Character is built in private. Your reputation is what people think you are, but your character is what God know you are. If you want to go the distance in life, focus more on character.

Be quick to listen, slow to speak, and slow to get angry.

Your 'Likes' impact their 'Life'

www.ingramcontent.com/pod-product-compliance
Lightning Source LLC
Chambersburg PA
CBHW062110220526
45471CB00010B/3675